24HR UNDER ATTACK

TOMMY DEFENDS THE FRONTLINE

24HR UNDER ATTACK

TOMMY DEFENDS THE FRONTLINE

ANDREW ROBERTSHAW

Find out more at http://andyrobertshaw.com

First published 2013

by Spellmount, an imprint of The History Press
The Mill, Brimscombe Port
Stroud, Gloucestershire, GL5 2QG
www.thehistorypress.co.uk

British Library Cataloguing in Publication Data.
A catalogue record for this book is available from the British Library.

ISBN 978 0 7524 8869 1

Typesetting and origination by The History Press
Printed in Europe

CONTENTS

ACKNOWLEDGEMENTS

This book is very much a team effort and I could not have completed it without the help, support and advice of a large group of people both in front of and behind the camera. I cannot list them all by name, but will do my best to express my thanks to as many as possible of the team. I have to start with the photographer Phil Erswell and his daughter Georgee, who provided double photographic coverage of the reconstruction sequences. They had to contend with live firing machine guns, pyrotechnics and a range of trench hazards that they would not normally encounter at even the most rowdy family wedding. Richard Knight provided a great deal of the kit in addition to appearing as a 'storm trooper'. I never thought that we would get that Bergmann sub machine gun out of his grip once it started firing. I am only sorry that not all of the uniform and equipment came from his business 'Khaki on Campaign'. The realism of some of the scenes required firing weapons and Ken Garside of Bapty Ltd spent a day on site with an arsenal of stunning machine guns. The majority of the 'troops' in the book are members of the 10th Essex, a re-enactment unit who are well known from their events in the United Kingdom and Western Front. Most re-enactors are wedded to 'their' regiment, but when I asked them to arrive without their battle insignia and badges, they did so to a man and were then transformed into temporary members of the King's Liverpool Regiment and in one case as a German. It has to be said that Craig Appleton was able to appear in the studio shots but managed to avoid anything in the trenches where he might have got wet! I think I was never so surprised as when I encouraged some shouting to make a scene more realistic to discover that the 'German' could actually speak the language. Other soldiers included Ross Barnwell, Dr Roger Payne and Neil McGurk, who is the only member of the team to appear in both *24hr Trench* and *24hr Under Attack*.

I needed a lot of support during the setting-up period and I really have to thank Steve Roberts and Mark Khan for all their hard work. As an ex-member of the Metropolitan Police Steve is used to breaking bad news and it was Steve who had to tell me that during the photography Roger had run over one of my original mess tins. I promised not to make a fuss about this, but putting it on paper has made me feel better. The tin was the only casualty of the entire project and I have to acknowledge that many of the participants felt uneasy about being photographed as 'the dead'. It was in the reason of taste that we decided not to use 'fake' blood. The point was made effectively and simply by posture. We all felt that there is a fine line between 'realism' and being gratuitous.

Finally, we all needed to be fed and once again, it was Diane Carpenter who produced a range of stews to original recipes.

The team of historians who helped to reconstruct these 24 hours under attack, using original war diaries and manuals.

FOREWORD

The Great War occurred at a time in history in which it was relatively simple to take photographs and even possible to make moving film, leading many people to believe that the events that occurred between 1914 and 1918 are well recorded and the experience of the men who fought on the frontline faithfully passed down to future generations. The reality is that as private cameras were officially forbidden in the British Army, and only a few official cameramen were at the front and even fewer movie cinematographers, the surviving record is, at best, partial. The reasons for this are easy to explain. The War Office restricted the number of officially sanctioned photographs and cameramen to manage cost and retain control. The photographs were taken and film recorded for reasons of propaganda rather than as a historical record of all aspects of the war. Censorship meant that many aspects of the war were not recorded and, in many cases, film and photographs that were deemed 'unsuitable' were destroyed. The nature of the fighting and threat from the enemy to the lives of the cameramen further restricted what could be recorded. Additionally those responsible for taking film or photographs of the war were looking for 'interesting' images, not the ordinary or mundane. Also, critically the nature of the equipment meant that cameras were heavy and cumbersome, difficult to focus and without the proliferation of lenses available to modern cameramen. Exposure times for still photographs could be long and film cameras were virtually impossible to zoom in and out, and panning shots were technically difficult. Although colour film was available for both still and movie cameras it was rarely used and the result of this is that the Great War is seen as being a monochrome conflict, although it was experienced by the participants in colour.

The consequence of all these limitations is that our record of even famous events in the Great War is limited to what can be seen as 'snapshots' of the conflict. The blanket coverage anticipated from the news today is absent, there is no balance to the recording of events and we are presented with fragments of the past. If it was possible to use every image made by a cameraman of a single day the cost would be prohibitive as museum archives charge a great deal for both the image and the licence to publish them. The limitations of the technology would mean that even if there were an unlimited budget there would only be a few good images to choose from or a few hundred feet of film. For this book, I wanted to cover the events of 24 hours as it affected the men of a single unit. In my previous book *24hr Trench* for a variety of reasons I had chosen the 1/5th King's Liverpool Regiment for my focus and it is to them that I return in this volume. To my knowledge, they were not photographed or filmed on the first day of the Battle of the Lys and it is therefore impossible to present any visual narrative account of their actions. It was therefore my intention to represent the actions of 9 April 1918 through recreation using modern cameras working with colour film to portray the battle from as many aspects as possible. This would allow me to get images

that would have been impossible in 1918 to illustrate the battle from the British and German points of view and to show the battle as it was experienced rather than as it is imagined today.

A reconstruction is a recreation of the original events and the most accurate re-enactment cannot, and should not attempt to, portray the level of hardship, fear and trauma experienced at the time. This is as true of a film or photographic reconstruction as it is for standard text or other interpretation of the events. We now live in a time when the last of the participants has passed away and we must use other forms of evidence to inform our understanding of the past. My intention in *24hr Under Attack* is to show as many aspects as possible of the experience of a small group of soldiers from 1/5th King's Liverpool Regiment over the 24 hours of 8 to 9 April 1918 as they faced the German offensive on the River Lys in Flanders. I have based the '24 Hours in Action' on their own accounts from the battle diaries. However, for reasons of taste I have avoided the graphic and potentially bloody recreation of the scenes of that day. I believe readers have sufficient good sense to realise that the worst events of that day are left to our imaginations without being gratuitously recreated for the camera. Having been present when the remains of soldiers who died in combat in the Great War have been discovered and on one occasion doing so myself, I can confirm that evidence of traumatic death is only slightly reduced by the passage of nearly 100 years. Death on the battlefield is random and produces horrific injuries that we do not have to see to imagine. It is arguable that this is censorship, much as was applied in the war itself, but my reason for doing this is not political, but good taste and the fact that not even the most faithful reconstruction can do justice to some aspects of real combat and that is not my intention. All I can hope is that the images and accompanying text herein can evoke the many facets of 24 hours in battle on the River Lys in April 1918, and that by so doing we can reach a greater understanding of how and why men operated in a certain way when under attack, and feel a greater empathy and respect for their experience.

The reconstruction of these 24 hours in action was shot in a specially reconstructed trench system, built by a team of historians and archaeologists in 2011 according to original trench manuals.

It is not possible, or desirable, to relive history, but historical reconstructions can help us to understand what happened and why, so that we might learn from it for the future. They can also help us to sort through the many myths and misconceptions that surround the Great War, so that we can get closer to the war as experienced, rather than as imagined in later books and films.

INTRODUCTION

One of the most pervasive myths of the Great War on the Western Front is that trench stalemate came about because of the nature of the weapons and defensive techniques in use when the war began. It is suggested that it was magazine-fed rifles, machine guns and long-range artillery combined with barbed wire that made open warfare impossible. The consequence of this level of firepower and difficulty in cutting through the barbed wire defences was that both sides 'dug in'. What followed, according to the myth, is that both sides fought an inconclusive and ultimately pointless war of attrition in which the Allies sometimes attacked and the Germans always defended. This argument fuels the opinion that the Great War was apparently futile and explains in a simple way why the Western Front was, apparently, static for so long.

The reality is that the war began with open manoeuvre warfare and would end the same way. In 1914, the German Army was able to advance hundreds of miles to the gates of Paris whilst under fire from the very weapons that apparently made this type of warfare impossible. Both sides were armed with the latest generation of rifles with smokeless ammunition, machine guns and an array of artillery with a higher rate of fire and longer range than anything that had been seen previously. Despite this, the German Army was able to make headway against stubborn French and British defence. The retreat from Mons, which took the British Army back over the River Marne, was mirrored elsewhere on the front. Only around fortresses did the German advance falter and, even then, heavy guns were able to breach even the most modern defences. Belgian fortifications crumbled and the advance continued. It was only at the point when the Eiffel Tower and hence the heart of Paris was in sight that this apparently inexorable process came to a halt. This was not due to the weight of firepower or improved Allied defences.

French soldiers 'digging in' mid-war. (Official photograph, *The Times History of the War, Vol. XVIII*, 1919)

The original caption for this contemporary drawing read: 'VERY LIKE A SERIES OF GROUSE-BUTTS! GERMAN BUSH-SCREENED SHELTER-TRENCHES AT THE BATTLE OF THE MARNE: Our illustration will help in giving one reason for the protracted nature of the fighting along the Aisne and why the Germans have been able to offer so tenacious a resistance. The way in which they literally dug themselves in everywhere, we see here: making elaborate shelter-trenches deep enough to cover men to their armpits, and enable them to fire on a

level with the ground, with emergency protection, further, against enfilade fire. To conceal the trenches leafy branches were planted in front so as to look like ordinary clumps of bushes, between the stems of which men fired, the smokeless powder used materially aiding the concealment. The visual effect of the bush cover at a little way off is well shown by the two trenches towards the centre of the picture, which are so screened.' This was just a foretaste of the Germans' prowess in defensive warfare. (From *The Illustrated War News, Vol. 1*, 1914)

It was the simple consequence of the shortage of manpower in the German Army that meant that they had insufficient men to offer a firm front to their opponents from Switzerland to the furthest northern extent of their forces. This was combined with the impossibility of supplying the most advanced forces over the captured territory from the German border. These forces were the ones on the outskirts of Paris and with victory in sight. Indeed, the logistics problem was critical. Although the German forces could rely on their railway system to deploy the army and to supply them to the end of the German railway network, beyond that destruction of the French and German railways meant that supplies had to be carried by horse-drawn wagons. This meant that despite the power of modern weapons, without logistical support that would have been familiar to Napoleon, further advance was impossible. It was all that the German supply chain could do to provide the food, fodder and ammunition for the forces where they were. Any further advance risked total collapse and potential defeat. In the period that followed, although both sides attempted to outflank the other through the open gap to the north in what was termed the 'Race to the Sea', it was clear to Germany that a rapid victory in the west was now an impossibility. Faced with a massive Russian army in the east which had completed mobilisation and which would threaten Berlin within weeks, the German high command had to find a way to both hold on to the captured territory and send troops east. They chose to 'dig in' on the most defensive and advantageous positions from Switzerland to the sea. This process had already begun, but now became a matter of policy. Germany could still win if Russia was speedily defeated and the entire available forces returned to the west. In the intervening time, Germany could hold on to the occupied areas of France and Belgium, which could provide a bargaining tool in the event of a negotiated peace. If the Allies wanted the areas of France and Belgium back, they would have to either fight for them or come to some agreement that suited Germany.

In this situation, Germany could afford to take a defensive stance, to construct an extensive system of trenches and other defences intended to absorb Allied attacks. If need be, as occurred in 1917 on the so-called Hindenburg Line, they could fall back to purpose-built fortifications, conceding to the enemy a little of the occupied ground whilst shortening their own frontline. All of this could be carried out at little expense to Germany as the resources of the occupied countries could be used with impunity. The reverse of this was a situation for the Allies in which they had to find a way to break the German defences in the west by an indirect approach. This explains the attempts to outflank the Western Front by supporting Russia and Italy and by mounting campaigns in Gallipoli against Turkey and at Salonika against Bulgaria. All of these campaigns ultimately failed and the war resolved itself to one of attrition on the Western Front as it became clear to the Allied politicians that there was no other military alternative. They would task their generals with wearing down the German opponent to a point at which the trench stalemate would collapse and the war would resume a final phase of 'open warfare'. This explains the nature of the war in the west from 1915 to the spring of 1918. The Allies launched increasingly large and sophisticated offensives using the new weapons of the war including gas, tanks, mining and artillery barrages whilst the Germans defended. This German 'philosophy of defence'

German heavy artillery. (French official photograph, *The Times History of the War, Vol. XVIII*, 1919)

British heavy artillery. (Official photograph, *The Times History of the War, Vol. XVIII*, 1919)

resulted from the stalemate of 1914 and circumstances in which the immediate German war aim, victory in the west, had failed.

The only occasion when the German Army went on the offensive during this period is the attack of February 1916 on the French fortress of Verdun. Various explanations of this campaign have been provided. These include a determination by the German Chief of Staff, Erich von Falkenhayn, to 'bleed France white' by inflicting so many casualties on her forces that the will to continue the war from the French people would end. The plan called for a German attack on Verdun that would draw in so many French defenders that they could be massacred. This loss of manpower would bring France to its knees, and rather than suffer further crippling losses it would, he suggested, capitulate and end the war in the west. This victory would then allow Germany to achieve a final conclusive victory against Russia and achieve all the territorial and other objectives, which were a vital war aim. Although debate continues about the justification for this risky strategy, the attack on Verdun was delivered on 21 February 1916. The battle raged until the autumn and despite the immense loss of life on both sides, proved to be as indecisive as the preceding period of stalemate. Neither side gained a strategic advantage from the fighting in which it is estimated that both sides lost over a third of a million casualties. By the autumn, the German Army was facing the hammer blows of the Anglo-French Somme battle that had begun in late June and was back on the defensive. The battle ended in November of that year and by that time Germany was incapable of mounting anything other than a defensive posture in the west. In February of 1917, the German Army was forced to withdraw to what the Allies called the Hindenburg Line, shortening the trenches manned by its soldiers, although ceding vast areas of lands that it had previously occupied.

The year 1917 was one of further Allied hammer blows in the west and the German Army lost more territory, although there were some successes. The news that America had declared war on Germany was only a few days old when the British and Canadian attack near Arras at Easter meant the loss of Vimy Ridge, although the vaunted French offensive under General Nivelle failed with terrible losses. The following month the British mines at Messines blew the German defenders from a ridge, which they had held since June 1914. Hardly had the dust settled when the Third Battle of Ypres, otherwise known as Passchendaele, began on the last day of July. Once again, the protracted and muddy struggle stretched into the early winter and only reached its culmination point when the village from which the battle took its name fell in November. If the Germans felt that these assaults had meant that the Allies were exhausted, they were proved incorrect by the Battle of Cambrai that began in the third week of November. Despite the use of over 400 tanks by the British, the Germans managed to stem the advance and counter-attacks pushed the British back, but with heavy losses on both sides. The battle struggled on into December and the year could have been considered a disaster for Germany had it not been for encouraging news from the Eastern Front. Racked by revolution and the large-scale collapse of its army, the Tsarist Russian forces were unable to continue the struggle against Germany and Austro-Hungary. An armistice was agreed in late December 1917 and although the peace treaty of Brest-Litovsk was not signed until March 1918, it was clear that Russia was out of the war. For Germany, this meant that their forces could go back on to the offensive using troops released from the east to achieve a final victory on the Western Front before the United States could field an effective army.

Fighting major battles in winter on the Western Front was out of the question and both sides knew that it would be the spring before the attack came. The question was now when and where would the blow fall?

By the early New Year of 1918, whilst the French pressed for an extension of the front held by the British and hence a reduction of their own line, both Allied armies were facing manpower shortages. Both of them were preparing to be attacked and doing what they could to husband resources of men and material ahead of the onslaught that would follow. The British placed their faith in new tactics, which consigned the old concept of fixed trench lines that were intended to hold when attacked to the dustbin. From now on, the defences consisted of deep defensive zones, which can be likened to a sponge in comparison to the previous eggshell of trenches. It was anticipated that an enemy attack would penetrate the lightly held outer defensive positions, but be absorbed in the depth of the battle zone and beaten back by strong counter-attacks. This new 'elastic defence' called for careful training and preparation specifically among junior officers and NCOs. However, short of men and bogged down in the routine of holding the line, working behind the lines and moving, meant that little time was left for training. What training there was only dealt with the basics of infantry skills as the influx of conscripts saw the ranks increasingly filled with under-trained men fresh from camps in the United Kingdom. Most units had some veterans, but very few were men of the pre-war regular army. Most were volunteers who had been civilians in 1914, but had achieved the status of veterans by the sheer act of survival.

Operation Michael: the Germans mobilise, 24 March 1918. (Bundesarchiv, Bild 104-0984A)

The question of where and when the German attack would be delivered was answered at precisely 04:40 on the morning of 21 March 1918. A barrage from nearly 6,500 pieces of artillery was unleashed on the front of the British Fifth and Third Armies south of the city of Arras. Operation Michael, under the command of General Ludendorff, had begun. Within hours, the German attack, using innovative artillery tactics and the extensive employment of 'storm troop' tactics, had broken through the battle zone. British casualties rose to over 100,000 and the reserves that were sent into battle appeared capable of slowing, but not stemming the enemy advance. Over the next week, the Allied commanders struggled to find sufficient men and guns to deal with the German advance on the Somme front toward Amiens.

The French General Foch was appointed as commander of the Allied armies – an act that relegated General Haig to a subordinate, but unified Allied command. As the German advance lost momentum, they launched a subsidiary operation, Mars, in the north of the existing bulge in the British lines. This attack failed, having come up against strong British defences.

By early April, it was clear that the initial German Operation Michael had failed to achieve total success and that Operation Mars had done little damage. However, General Ludendorff still had substantial uncommitted forces available. These fresh divisions could be used to attack where they would do the greatest damage. British military intelligence, on the other hand, was aware that they had few uncommitted men to deal with a new offensive and appealed for assistance from the French to provide a reserve and relieve some units that were already in action. This request was refused and on the eve of the third German offensive – Operation Georgette – there were few reserve forces available, although the decision by the British government to release for active service trained men from 18½ years of age, rather than 19, provided a pool of fresh, if inexperienced, manpower. These would be supplemented by men 'combed out' from depots and training schools who could be used as reinforcements for existing formations. In both cases, however, this process was piecemeal and the new men had little time to become familiar with their new comrades and the situation before they were thrust into action. And so it would be a battered and under-strength British Army that faced the forthcoming German offensive.

THE BRITISH INFANTRYMAN IN 1918

On the declaration of war with Germany in August 1914, the soldiers of the British Expeditionary Force (BEF) arriving at the French ports were armed and trained for open warfare. Using skills that had been, largely, developed from the experience of the Boer War, 1899–1902, and other colonial conflicts, it was intended that virtually every man in a British infantry battalion (which consisted of over a thousand men) was armed with the latest pattern of Short Magazine Lee-Enfield (SMLE) rifle and bayonet. Pre-war training was intended to ensure that the British infantry would be able to generate a rapid rate of very accurate fire. He carried between 120 and 150 rounds (bullets) of ammunition for his personal weapon and was expected to be able to fire at least fifteen well-aimed rounds in a minute. This firepower was supplemented by the unit's machine guns, Maxim or Vickers guns, which fired the same bullet as the rifles but at a rate of fire of up to 600 rounds per minute. The intention was that the combination of weapons would allow the infantryman to close with and dislodge enemy soldiers in the attack or to keep them at a distance and defeat them in the open if the enemy mounted an offensive action.

Although it is a subject of debate as to whether the German soldiers at Mons in Belgium really mistook the accurate rifle fire of British soldiers for multiple machine guns, the weapons and tactics of the BEF worked. The BEF was able to slip away from the enemy advance and inflict significant casualties upon their opponents. The retreat from Mons brought the British Army across the Marne and for a brief period it looked as if Paris could fall. With the German advance halted and rapid victory beyond the grasp of its forces, the decision to dig in meant that both sides went into trenches. In this type of warfare, the skilled infantryman armed with an accurate rifle could do little damage to his opponent and even the machine gun could not hit targets in sandbagged trenches. Increasingly, to stem the casualties, artillery and the infantry had to look for new weapons better suited to the conditions in which they found themselves. Mortars, used in siege warfare, reappeared, as did grenades, which could be thrown from the open into a trench or from a trench against troops in the open. Some of these early weapons were improvised and frankly 'Heath Robinsonesque' in design, probably more dangerous to the user than his target. However, new patterns of commercially manufactured and tested mortars and grenades, called bombs by the British, appeared and by 1915, the inventory of every infantry unit included these new weapons. The standard pattern of grenade became the No. 5 and this featured a segmented iron casing and was ignited by means of the removal of a safety pin and ring, which released the striker lever held in the thrower's hand. Five seconds later the bomb detonated scattering the fragments of iron casing in all directions. This grenade proved to be reliable, effective and easily mass-produced. However, one limitation of even the best 'bomb' was its range of only 35 yards. A soldier could only throw a heavy iron grenade tens of yards and he frequently needed a greater reach. The solution was the rifle grenade. Various patterns were tried, some of which worked and others which were highly dangerous to anyone within range. However, the pattern finally selected was the No. 23 grenade, which could be propelled from the standard rifle by means of a strong blank cartridge. This pushed a rod that was screwed into the base of the special bomb up the barrel of the weapon. To prevent the premature ignition of the bomb it was retained until fired inside a steel attachment that fitted on to the muzzle of the rifle. Once the firer was ready, he removed the safety pin and then fired the blank. As the bomb left the attachment the striker lever was released and this ignited and seven seconds later, two more than the hand grenade, the bomb would detonate whether on the ground or still in the air. This air burst capacity made the rifle bomb a threat to men in the open or in a trench and the range of up to 90 yards was impressive and effective. By late 1917, a more complex system using a solid discharger cup meant that the No. 36 grenade could be fired up to 210 yards.

If the various forms of grenade were novel so was the adoption by the British Army of the Lewis gun. This relatively light 'automatic rifle', as it was designated, had a magazine of just forty-seven rounds and was not capable of the sustained fire of the Vickers machine gun. It was, however, air cooled by comparison with the water-cooled Vickers and therefore lighter and more portable. The initial scale out of these Lewis guns saw one or two per battalion, but this increased so rapidly that by October 1915 it was possible to take the Vickers machine guns out of all infantry battalions and form them into the Machine Gun Corps. This meant that those machine guns left to the battalion had to be used in a different manner than previously. The Lewis gun lacked the range and indirect fire capacity of the Vickers but worked well as a line-of-sight weapon.

By 1916, all infantry battalions had a mixture of weapons: the rifle and bayonet, the bomb, the rifle bomb and Lewis gun. Before the Somme battle, a number of experiments were conducted to determine how this range of weapons could be used in combination. Some units experimented with bombing companies, a form of organisation that harked back to the Grenadier Company of the eighteenth-century infantry, in which they put all trained bombers into a single company rather than dispersing them across the battalion. Some units tried massing Lewis guns at company level whilst others shared them out amongst the small sub-units, platoons. The harsh lessons of the Somme demonstrated that the use of the weapons available to the British battalion failed to make the best advantage of the features of each one either individually or in combination. However, new French tactics using very similar combinations of weapons had proved to be very successful. The result was the issue of new training instructions to units drawing heavily on the French experience, but adapted to the skills and weapons of the British soldier. The new manual SS 143, *The Platoon in Offensive Action*, changed the emphasis from the company of around 200 soldiers to the platoon, of around thirty. Within the platoon four roles were developed, as illustrated below.

A section of snipers, scouts and bayonet men.

This section is armed with standard rifles and relies for fire effect upon the SMLE; however, in hand-to-hand combat the men in this section are the bayonet experts.

 The 'typical' British infantryman of 1917 equipped with his SMLE rifle.

2 The early use of the bayonet dates back to the seventeenth century and it still forms part of the British infantry's equipment today. The concept of bayonet fighting was that it would enable an infantryman to take the battle to the enemy at close quarters. When not in use, the bayonet was carried in a scabbard on his webbing to allow the infantryman easy access to the weapon.

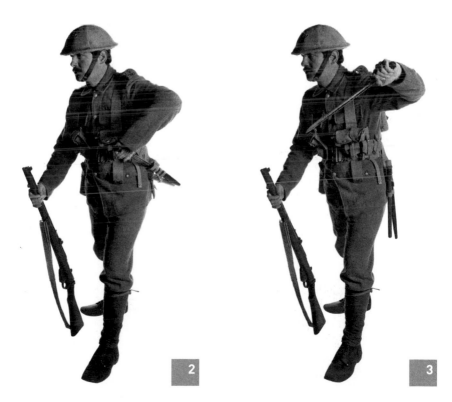

2   3

3 The bayonet could be used on its own, although this was very rare, or attached to the soldier's rifle, depending on the proximity to the enemy or whether the soldier had time to prepare himself in advance to attack. The use of the bayonet as a multi-purpose knife became more common during the Great War, especially as this allowed greater flexibility in trench-raiding parties, where having it fixed to the rifle made the whole weapon too cumbersome and unwieldy to negotiate the small passages in which the men might find themselves. Some soldiers had bayonets cut down to create fighting knives, specifically for raiding.

4+5 Commonly, photographs from the Great War show soldiers 'going over the top' with fixed bayonets in the method of a traditional bayonet charge and this method was certainly a key part of the infantryman's training. However, the advance with men at the 'high port' with the weapon across the chest and every man in line became a thing of the past by 1917.

6 The concept of fixing bayonets to rifles was centred round the notion of increasing the infantryman's 'reach' to the enemy. With the introduction of the shorter pattern Lee-Enfields it became necessary to increase the length of the bayonet blade, the sword bayonet, in order to maintain this ideal. No one wants to be out reached by an opponent in a bayonet fight.

7-14 An infantryman's training would have included the various ways in which the bayonet could be used to attack and defend a position. Many new recruits would find bayonet training psychologically quite difficult as the notion of 'making contact' with the enemy at such close range was something that they probably hoped they would never have to face. The training was centred in overcoming the natural response to the thought of stabbing an opponent at close quarters. Training included techniques for fighting opponents above a soldier if an attacker tried to get into a trench.

4

5

6

A section of bombers.

Using the No. 5 or possibly No. 36 grenades. Although there was a limited number of trained bombers, who carried rifles slung, the rest of the section carried additional bombs in boxes, canvas buckets with a drawstring cover or additional haversacks. All are rifle armed. The section can combine rifle fire with the ability to bomb an objective if they can get within 20 or so yards.

 The bomber; note the haversack on his front for easy access to his grenades (bombs).

15

16

17

17a

17b

18

18-20 Once the bomber pulled the pin, it was vital that the grenade was dispatched as quickly as possible to avoid injury to himself and his fellow soldiers. This type of 'bombing' not only required a good throwing arm and aim, but also necessitated the bomber being within throwing distance of the enemy, making it a hazardous job. The bomb has to be thrown from behind cover into the open or from cover, such as a trench, into the open, as the fragments will travel further than a man can throw it.

19

The rifle bombing section.

In this section there would not be more than two men firing grenades at any one time; the remainder carry additional grenades in haversacks, etc. All are rifle armed and can hit targets up to 200 yards away if equipped with the latest discharger cups and grenades. The men not firing rifle bombs can operate with rifles to provide additional firepower.

21

22

21 The rifle bomber, loaded down with his rifle and fixed bayonet, as well as his 'bomb bag'.

22 Working from the shelter of a trench or shell hole, the rifle bomber checks his target using a small trench periscope. Accuracy was a vital skill for the rifle bomber and his concealment would determine the success of the action.

23+24 Preparing to load the grenade or 'bomb' into the rifle. Note the rod that allows the grenade to be propelled into the air when the energy from the blank cartridge hits it.

25 The pin at the base of the grenade slides into the rifle barrel and the grenade itself is held in place by a steel ring attached to the top of the rifle barrel. This also retains the fly off lever once the pin has been removed.

26 It was important to ensure that the grenade was securely fitted into the rifle so as to avoid mistakes.

27-31 The rifle bomber prepares and loads the special heavy blank cartridge into the rifle, which will propel the grenade into the air, giving it the momentum to travel a much greater distance than the bomber alone could throw it.

32 The rifle is now fully loaded and prepared to fire; this combination of rifle and grenade would prove a deadly addition to the infantryman's arsenal as the war progressed. The rifle bomber was considered the 'howitzer of trench warfare'.

25

25a

27

28

29

30

31

The Lewis gun section.

This usually consisted of two guns and eight or so men. The remaining men in the section carry ammunition pans in canvas buckets or the circular pouches worn front and rear of the wearer. All are rifle armed apart from the Lewis No. 1s who carry a pistol as a personal weapon. As in other sections, all the men in the section can use their rifles and are trained to replace any casualties.

33

24hr Under Attack: Tommy Defends the Frontline

33+34 The air-cooled Lewis gun weighed 28lb (12.7kg), making it lighter than the Vickers machine gun and thus it was possible for a single soldier to carry it.

35 Although designed to enable a single soldier to carry it and fire it, Lewis gun teams worked in pairs, with the Number Two carrying his own SMLE and the drum magazines for the Lewis over his shoulder, alongside his respirator around his neck. The firer, or Number One, of the Lewis carries a pistol as a weapon of personal defence should the machine gun jam or run out of ammunition.

37

38

36 One of the key jobs of the Lewis gunner's partner would be to check that the magazines were fully and correctly loaded, ensuring that a rapid rate of fire could be sustained. The magazines have an open bottom and dirt and dust was a constant problem.

37-40 He would then ensure that the circular drum magazine was tightly fitted to the gun's body. The gun's rate of fire was 500–600 rounds per minute and it was surprisingly effective, becoming adopted throughout the British Army and was still in use in the Second World War.

39

40

41 The Lewis gun team would work closely together, with the Number Two carefully watching the rounds being discharged and ensuring that the magazine could be changed quickly. Once a new magazine is loaded the Number Two taps the firer on the shoulder with an open hand to indicate that he can start firing.

42 Although the Lewis was commonly fired from a bipod with a gun team in place, the relative lightness of the weapon allowed for it to be fired unconventionally as here. Being air cooled and light, the Lewis made an ideal machine gun with which to arm aircraft.

41

Awthorty

[S.S. 143.]

O.B./1919/T.
40/W.O./5868.

FOR OFFICIAL USE ONLY.

THIS Document is the property of H.B.M. Government, and the information in it is not to be communicated, either directly or indirectly, to the Press or any person not holding an official position in His Majesty's Service.

THE TRAINING AND EMPLOYMENT OF PLATOONS 1918

ISSUED BY THE GENERAL STAFF.

This publication cancels:—

The original edition of S.S. 143, "Instructions for the Training of Platoons for Offensive Action, 1917" (February, 1917).

"The Organization of an Infantry Battalion" (O.B./1919: dated 7.2.17) and "The Normal Formation for the Attack" (S.S. 144, February, 1917)—both issued together in April, 1917, under 40/W.O./3995.

February, 1918.

Wt. W 5642. PP 1386. 170,000. 3/18 U.P.O. **(E 2732)**

These new ways of operating meant that from the early months of 1917 a British platoon had a mix of weapons that allowed it to cope with a range of potential situations whether in the attack or in defence. Critically, unlike their German opponents who increasingly put reliance upon groups of highly trained and well-equipped 'storm troops' at the expense of the bulk of their forces, all British platoons were expected to be able to use the new tactics and would receive the weapons and equipment they required to do so. The effect of these tactics was first demonstrated at Arras in Easter 1917 and the capture of Vimy Ridge by the Canadians can, in part, be attributed to the use of the SS 143. This success was followed by the Battle of Messines in June, an occasion when the use of mines and the now well-established tactics meant that the Germans lost a position which they had held since 1914. If the battles that followed at Ypres, the Battle of Passchendaele and then at Cambrai in November were not so successful, this can be attributed to the German response and their use of new tactics and defensive techniques. However, with the situation so changed by the late winter of 1918 the question remained, how well would British tactics work in defence?

The new manual of February 1918, *The Training and Employment of Platoon, 1918*, uses just one page of the nineteen-page booklet to concentrate on 'The Principles of Defence'. One aspect of this page is to stress that 'The soul of defence lies in offence; passive resistance by fire alone may check, but it cannot overthrow the enemy'. In May 1918, on the Lys front, it remained to be seen whether the men of the 55th Division would be capable of defence, let alone offence.

14.—Principles of Defence.

1. A principle which underlies all defensive tactics is that positions should be organized in depth, arranged chequerwise, so as to bring as much mutually supporting fire to bear as possible.

This organization should have for its object the maximum development of fire over all ground which may be crossed by an enemy in the course of his attack. The fire of rifles and Lewis guns, controlled by Section Commanders, has been proved again and again to be a decisive factor; wherever possible, Lewis guns should be sited in flanking positions from which they can develop their maximum fire effect on the deep, dense target then presented by an attacking enemy.

2. Organizing a position for defence, or, in the term frequently used, "consolidating" a position, does not *necessarily* imply digging; though the digging of a trench usually is a means of securing both fire positions and protection, positions may be, and in open warfare often are, organized to resist attack in a very few minutes. The first essentials are the occupation of mutually supporting tactical points, screened as far as possible from artillery fire, and the creation of fire positions. When possible, the wiring of these should always precede digging, and the wire should be sited in accordance with the fields of fire—that is to say, it should never be put out haphazard in front of the positions occupied, but should run along lines selected with a view to checking the enemy where he can be caught by flanking fire or caused to bunch at some spot commanded by rifles or Lewis guns. Practice in the siting of wire with regard to the positions occupied and in putting it out rapidly will never be wasted.

3. The occupation of a forward defensive position does not in the first instance demand a continuous line; it may be necessary at a later stage to link up the positions to facilitate command and communication, but as long as the element of surprise is present, short lengths of fire position arranged according to the lie of the ground, each accommodating a section and supporting one another by cross and converging fire, will be less conspicuous, and therefore less exposed to shell fire, and more effective in breaking up the hostile attack. Behind the barrier presented by these the main line of resistance can then be organized.

4. The soul of defence lies in offence; passive resistance—that is, resistance by fire alone may check, but it cannot overthrow the enemy. Commanders must be ready to take the initiative, both to use the bayonet, when necessary, and to restore the fight if any part of the position is overwhelmed. Every situation must as far as possible be foreseen and arrangements made in advance so that it may be met *immediately*.

The ground over which immediate counter-attacks will be made must be reconnoitred beforehand, and every Section Commander given clearly to understand the rôle which his section may be called upon to fulfil. The unexpected is the rule in war, but if every Commander realizes that he is directly responsible for making in advance detailed plans for every likely event the unexpected may be turned to advantage, and confusion, loss of time, and consequent failure avoided. It is frequently possible to practise counter-attacks over the actual ground on which they may have to be delivered: where this can be done, it is the best security that every man will know exactly where to go and what to do. A local counter-attack to be successful must be delivered immediately after the enemy's capture of a position. If he is given time to organize it for defence, it will ordinarily be necessary to arrange for a methodical counter-attack at a later date.

5. Every Commander must not only guard his flanks and keep in touch with neighbouring units, but be ready either to co-operate in a counter-attack or to throw back a defensive flank in the event of a neighbouring unit being driven from its position. He will never withdraw from a position without being ordered to do so; by holding on he may enable the whole position to be restored.

6. The above principles apply to defence as much in open as in trench warfare, but in open warfare still greater importance attaches to the personal reconnaissance of the Commander, the work of reconnoitring patrols, and the selection and organization of fire positions.

7. In all warfare, both in the attack and in the defence, in open and in trench warfare, Commanders must study their system of communications and keep their immediate superiors and neighbouring Commanders fully and frequently informed of the situation; they must not refrain from sending back word because they have nothing particular to report; this very fact may be of the first importance. No possible means of keeping up communication should be neglected. Tactical exercises will be carried out by Company, Platoon, and Section Commanders, in which the importance of rendering reports as to their position and the tactical situation should be emphasized.

THE EVE OF BATTLE

The 55th Division was stationed in the Ypres Salient from October 1916 until the end of September 1917. In that time the division held the line from Wietje in the north to just south of Railway Wood. Units alternated between the frontline and reserve, and were able to enjoy what began as a 'quiet' sector by comparison with the Somme. The division had time to become familiar with this sector and on 31 July it attacked on this frontage at what was the Third Battle of Ypres, later called the Battle of Passchendaele. By the time the 55th Division was withdrawn from the attack, on 4 August, they had successfully obtained their objectives and taken thirty German officers and 600 Other Ranks prisoner. However, casualties had been heavy. By the time the division was relieved on 4 August, it had lost 168 officers and 3,384 Other Ranks killed, wounded and missing.

After a period of rest the division was committed to virtually the same sector and objectives on 20 September. This second attack was a success, as was the repulse of the German counter-attack, but once again casualties were heavy. By the time the division left the line for the second time it had suffered a further 2,730 casualties. The move that followed took the division out of the Ypres Salient and south to Cambrai in preparation for the major use of tanks in the battle that commenced on 20 November.

The role of the division in this battle was diversionary and intended to prevent the Germans from sending troops north to reinforce the forces contesting the main British attack toward Cambrai. Using a combination of dummy troops and tanks, chemical weapons and incendiaries, the enemy frontline was attacked on part of the divisional frontage. This attack was costly but appeared to have inflicted casualties on the enemy and to have contained German troops that could have been otherwise used elsewhere. As the main battle developed at Cambrai and the Germans mounted what proved to be

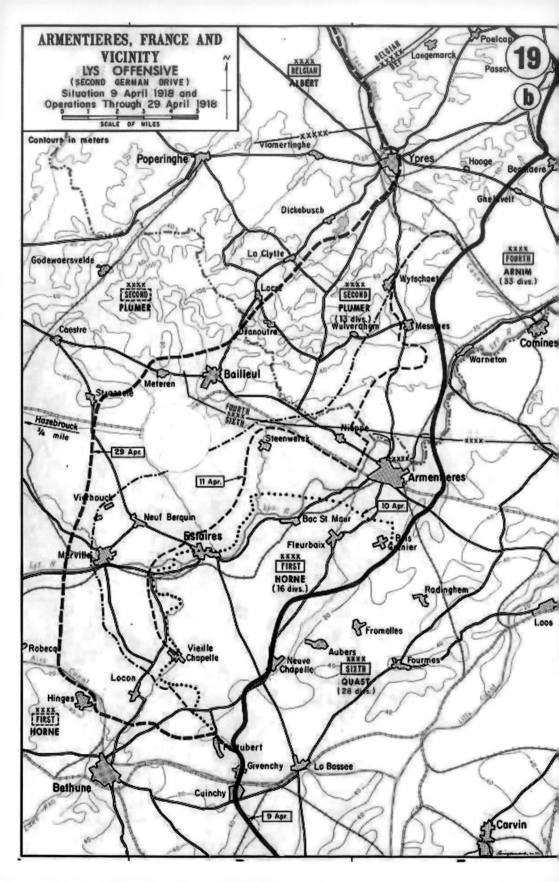

a successful counter-attack, the division was given responsibility for an increased frontline despite evidence that the enemy were preparing to mount their own attack. This came at 07:00 on 30 November when a heavy enemy bombardment fell on the whole front and at around 08:15 an infantry attack was mounted. In the fighting that followed, one brigade of the division, the 164th, was severely handled by the German attackers. Thick fog led to confusion and by mid-morning the division, which was attempting to hold a front of nearly 7 miles, found itself outflanked. British units to the north of the division had been pushed back by the strong German counter-attack and despite heavy casualties the northern battalions of the 55th Division attempted to hold on to its frontline position. Elsewhere units were more successful in repulsing enemy attacks and reinforcements were soon on their way from the division and other uncommitted units that had been held in reserve. By mid-afternoon the situation had begun to settle down and during the latter half of the afternoon the position had begun to stabilise, although there was still anxiety about the northern flank. A British counter-attack on the morning of 1 December with tank support was carried out on the northern front by two brigades of cavalry. These fresh troops met with little success and suffered heavy casualties, which indicates the fighting qualities of the German troops who had mounted the initial attack. The division remained in the area, although with responsibility for a much-reduced frontage, and was finally relieved on 6/7 December.

Out of the line, the infantry were moved to a rest area and given time to absorb reinforcements before being sent north to the area of Givenchy-Festubert on the last day of the year. Although the division considered itself to have done well, there was criticism of its performance and in the period when the men were out of the line a good deal of time was employed in training, especially rifle 'musketry'. During the time the division was out of the line, an order was received that the number of battalions in a division was to be reduced to nine

Map showing the German Lys Offensive, 1918. (United States Military Academy, reproduced from WikiCommons)

from the existing twelve. This came into force on 31 January and had the effect of greatly reducing the manpower available to the divisional commander. The only compensation was gradually improving firepower as the number of Lewis guns continued to increase.

The division took up its allotted place in the line between the La Bassée and Givenchy on 15 February. Here the 55th found itself to be the most northerly of the units in the British 1st Corps sector. To the north was the Portuguese 2nd Division. However, even though the division was back in the line it did not mean an end to relentless training. The divisional commander, Major-General Sir Hugh Jeudwine, had strong views on the division's preparation and clear orders were given as to what was expected from all ranks. Men were expected to be physically fit and to fire at least five rounds per day, later on progressing to ten or more. They were tested as to the speed with which they could man their fire positions from any dugout or place of safety. It was made clear that every platoon was expected to be a fighting unit capable of attacking or resisting without the support of others. Great emphasis was placed on the use of the rifle, bayonet and Lewis gun. Exercises were carried out to ensure that officers and NCOs were thoroughly familiar with their position in the line, the location of ammunition and stores and the means of communication to be used in all circumstances. The overall intention was to produce troops who knew what was expected of them, could generate the greatest possible volume of fire for their numbers, and that all ranks had confidence in their ability to contribute to the battle. All of these skills were to be required in the fighting that was to come that April.

One critically important factor in the fighting of April was the nature of the British defence system. As previously touched on, the techniques of trench warfare were constantly evolving and during the course of the war the depth, style and layout of trench systems were adapted in response to new weapons and enemy tactics. By 1918, the simple system of frontline trenches with support at some distance to the rear had been replaced by something that was far more sophisticated and subtle. In the old method of defence it was intended for the enemy to be defeated as he advanced across No Man's Land and the frontline was regarded as a crust that should not be pierced without imminent defeat. Should the enemy get into the frontline counter-attacks were required to eject the invader. These tactics meant that the frontline had to be heavily garrisoned and the inevitability of counter-attacks ensured that an opponent could inflict heavy casualties on a defender because he would know where his main effort would be directed. Artillery could be used to prepare for the attack, inflicting heavy casualties on the defenders and even greater casualties when their reserves attempted to advance against the captured area of trenches. This led to the attrition at Verdun and then again on the Somme. First the French and then the Germans lost heavily as they attempted to recapture ground taken in the initial enemy assault. All too frequently the line stabilised with little to show for the effort on both sides, other than dead and wounded in similar proportions. By 1917 German policy changed and Allied attacks found the frontline weakly held and any successful breakthrough to the attackers out of sight or range of their own supporting artillery. At this point, with the attackers deep in the German defence zone, their counter attack troops with artillery support could inflict heavy casualties on the isolated and vulnerable Allies who had entered a 'killing zone'.

By 1918, British defences manned by the 55th Division consisted of a frontline that was similarly thinly held. In support was a second line, called in this area the 'Village Line'. This consisted of machine-gun posts and defended localities some of which, based on the ruined villages, were referred to as 'Keeps'. Running behind the 'Village Line' and parallel with both that and the frontline was the final area of defence. This series of defended positions was the 'Battle Line' and the area between that and the frontline was up to 8 kilometres deep. What this represented was a defensive 'sponge' intended to absorb an attacker in a maze of interlocking defences into which he could advance but not break through. This at least was the theory; it remained to be seen whether it would work against the new German artillery tactics and 'storm troops'. One complicating factor was that all the planned defences were far from complete. What was required was time to construct the new defences in depth, lay the barbed wire and prepare the troops for their new tactics. Although intensive

THE PLATOON

Taking an average strength of 36 and H.Q. 4.

(Showing 2 Platoons in 2 Waves, with the right the outer flank).

FORMATION FOR TRENCH TO TRENCH ATTACK.

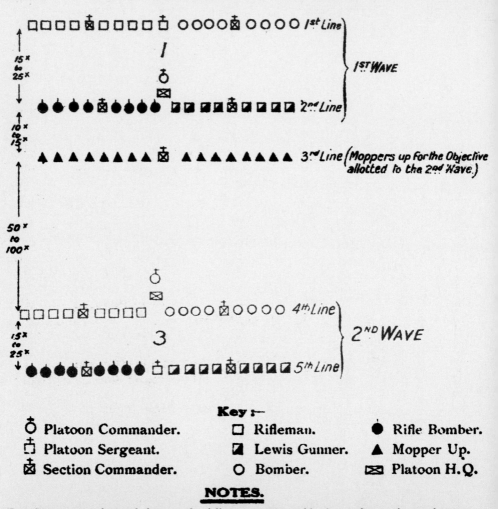

Key :—

♂ Platoon Commander.	☐ Rifleman.	● Rifle Bomber.
♁ Platoon Sergeant.	◪ Lewis Gunner.	▲ Mopper Up.
⊠ Section Commander.	○ Bomber.	⊠ Platoon H.Q.

NOTES.

Two Platoons are depicted showing the different positions of leaders in first and second waves.

The Platoon is the unit in the assault, moves in One Wave of two lines and has one definite objective

Every man is a rifleman and a bomber, and in the assault, with the exception of the No. 1 and No. 2 of Lewis Gun, fixes his bayonet. Men in rifle sections must be trained either to the Lewis Gun or Rifle Bomb.

Bombing and Lewis Gun Sections are on the outer flank of Platoons.

In assembly the distance between lines and waves may conveniently be reduced to lessen the danger of rear waves being caught in enemy barrage, the distance being increased when the advance takes place.

"Moppers up" follow the second line of a wave and precede the unit for which they are to mop up. If the numbers are large they must be found from a different Company or Battalion. Small numbers are preferably found from the unit for which they are to mop up. They must carry a distinctive badge and have their own Commander.

(12605) Wt W16056/9527 SPL 44M 3/17 H & J. Ld
(14536) Wt W151/9631 . 75,000 4/17 H & J, Ld

G.S.
O.B. No. 1919/T

TRENCH TO TRENCH ATTACK

PLATOON IN 1st WAVE
MEETING A POINT OF RESISTANCE.

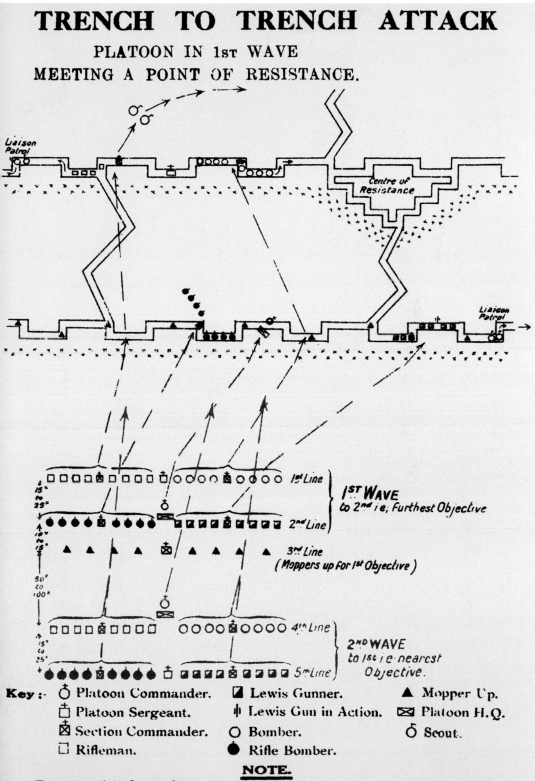

Key :-

Platoon Commander.	Lewis Gunner.	Mopper Up.
Platoon Sergeant.	Lewis Gun in Action.	Platoon H.Q.
Section Commander.	Bomber.	Scout.
Rifleman.	Rifle Bomber.	

NOTE.

The position of the Commander.

The Rifle Bombs and Lewis gun fire and rifle fire are obtaining superiority over the enemy's fire.

The bombers and riflemen have gone straight above ground to their objective, where they are turning the flank of the centre of resistance.

The use of scouts and liaison patrols.

The "Moppers up" are guarding the entrances to dugouts and communication trenches.

training continued, the division was now in the line and there were many demands on the men in the weeks ahead.

Indeed, the division had not been in the line long before the enemy decided to try out the preparations made by their opponents. German raids on 17 February and 7 March caused some casualties but both attacks were driven off. The later raid did not go unpunished. At 05:00 on the following morning, 18 March, the 1/5th King's Own Lancashire Regiment mounted a raid on the enemy lines. This large-scale raid consisted of a company of infantry and a small group of Royal Engineers. The raiders penetrated the German front and support lines but no enemy troops were encountered. This disappointing result was offset by a raid by the same battalion in the early morning of 25 March. On this occasion, nine enemy prisoners were captured together with a machine gun. In the days that followed the divisional front was, once again, extended and the 166th Brigade was ordered to take over a section of frontline. This order was countermanded on the night of 6/7 April and the brigade was put into divisional reserve. This decision was to have far-reaching consequences in the days ahead.

By early April news had spread of the initial German offensive in the west, Operation Michael, which was launched against General Gough's Fifth Army on 21 March 1918. This thrust, which was aimed at Amiens across the old Somme battlefield and was supported by nearly 5,500 artillery pieces, was unleashed on unprepared and undermanned British defences. Within days, more than 100,000 British troops were lost and for a period of days, it appeared possible that the British could be split from their French allies. Once again, Paris was under threat and British and French troops were poured in to stabilise the position. This was achieved, just, and with one attack running out of steam the German mastermind General Ludendorff launched a second attack, Operation Mars, against the British Third Army near Arras on 28 March. Although it failed, British intelligence indicated that the Germans had sufficient uncommitted troops to launch further attacks if they chose to do so. This was inevitable and the question was then where and when would this fall? Intelligence suggested the northern front in the area of Lens. Requests by Haig for further French support to take pressure off the over-committed British armies was turned down by Foch. As late as

8 April, Haig was still asking for French troops to take over the Ypres Salient to provide him a reserve of some sort. This was, again, refused and an undermanned British force awaited the expected German attack which they had codenamed 'Georgette'.

The front remained ominously quiet and on the night of 6 April, gas was fired into the enemy's trenches. It was, however, impossible to work out what results this might have had because even on the night of 8/9 April a patrol from the division that entered the German frontline found the trenches unoccupied. The next day was established as to be the day on which the Portuguese Brigade, next to 1/5th King's, would be relieved. Everything was in place for this to occur on the evening of the 9th. Events, however, prevented this from happening quite as intended. The date of 9 April was going to be a momentous one for 1/5th, but their new neighbours would not be welcome.

24 HOURS IN ACTION
8/9 APRIL 1918

Sleep is hard to come by, but rest is essential to ensure that you can spring into action when needed or are ready to take your turn on sentry duty or trench repairs.

22:45

As the coldest part of the night approaches the men from No. 3 Section, 15 Platoon, D Company, the 1/5th King's struggle to stay warm. The ten men in the section were divided into threes shortly before stand-to the previous evening. Now one-third takes it in turn to rest wherever they can in the trench as they are off duty for an hour. Of the others, some stand sentry, peering over the parapet with rifle and fixed bayonet in case of an enemy raid. The remainder work on the defences or other maintenance tasks that need to be carried out in the trench. The work is hard, but the men have found that it is a good way to warm up after their turn on 'sentry go' and the rest makes more sense after an hour of hard activity. Sleep is impossible, although a few men manage to doze sitting on the fire step close to a brazier or tucked up in one of the 'funk hole' shelters that dot the front face of the trench. Everyone is muddy and fed-up. This is their last night in this position and all are looking forward to the arrival of their relief, allowing them to take their turn behind the lines, resting and training.

On this night, that relief cannot come too soon. Not just because of the flooding, the cloying mud and biting cold of March, but because all ranks know that a German assault is due. Quite where and when is uncertain, but based on the experience of counter-attack the division received at Cambrai the previous November, not being in the frontline when it happens appears very attractive. Unfortunately despite great secrecy by the Germans, the signs of an impending assault on their front appear all too obvious. Unexplained noises indicating equipment being moved into position and artillery fire on specific targets all indicate 'something brewing'.

Others try to grab a few minutes' rest by the warmth of the brazier.

Men take it in turns to keep watch and the platoon sergeant oversees the platoon's activities. This time of waiting could feel endless, staring out into the darkness of No Man's Land, occasionally punctuated by a Very flare or unidentified sound from across the trenches. At this point, not knowing who was opposite them or what the morning might hold, the men are focussed on getting through the night and receiving the expected relief at the end of their time in the frontline.

23:00

A small group of men from 1/5th King's Liverpool Regiment are taking it in turns to get ready for a party that will start at midnight. Unlike most parties, this one will be both difficult and dangerous. The men have all volunteered to be part of a 'raiding party' that will attempt to enter the German frontline to discover who they are facing, and what, if anything, is being prepared. This information might be vital in the next few days or hours. A prisoner, or at least his identity tags or pay book if he does not survive, will reveal the information about the enemy unit. From that intelligence can work out whether they are a first-rate assault unit, or perhaps second rate, only fit to hold a position. The former would indicate a forthcoming attack, the latter the potential for this being a 'quiet sector' for at least a few more days.

23:10

The raiders get to work removing anything that would identify them if they were captured or left behind wounded, dead or a prisoner. Pockets are emptied of all pay books and letters, insignia is removed and identity tags go into the sandbag that will be left behind. All being well, the men will retrieve their own items on their return. If they fail to return these will be sent to next of kin at home. It is a sobering moment and reminds them all that they may not all be 'coming back'.

The raiders place their pay books and other identification in a haversack to hopefully reclaim later on their safe return. They are going looking for information about the enemy and do not want to give them a 'present' of intelligence should they be killed or captured in the raid.

23:20

The raiders have already discarded helmets, noisy equipment and webbing and replaced this with simple belts and a mixture of balaclava helmets and cap comforters intended to both disguise their faces and keep them warm. With most of the raiders clothed in dark wool, light-coloured hands and faces will betray them even in the dark. They begin to apply cork burnt in candle flames to the back of hands and faces. Boot polish would work well, but there is not much need for this product in the trenches, but some of the officers are known to have the odd bottle of wine so corks are easier to come by. Some of the men compare themselves with minstrels in the pre-war music halls and some manage to fool about to ease their nerves a little.

A cork placed in the candle flame provides the 'blacking' that the men need to disguise their faces.

s the men apply their war paint, the strangeness of the evening's activities is beginning to dawn on them. rench raids, although a part of trench life, are not an everyday occurrence and the idea of going across No Man's and and purposefully into the trenches on the other side, potentially straight into a waiting enemy bayonet, is ndoubtedly daunting.

23:30

The raiders select their weapons. Rifles and machine guns have little use once they enter the enemy trenches. Although the covering parties on the flanks of the raid will be conventionally armed, the raiders need weapons for silent, if possible, fighting in the confined space of the trenches. Clubs, knives and pistols are the weapons of choice and everyone has a spare in case of a jammed round in a pistol or other problem. Weapons are on lanyards or cords so that a dropped weapon will not be lost. No one wants to confront a German defender unarmed.

23:40

The last act before the raiders leave the dugout is a run through of the plan. The men are briefed on where they will meet in case of a problem, what the emergency signal and password is, and how far they can go into the enemy lines in the time available. With the approval of the commanding officer, the medical officer has provided a rum jar and the raiders take it in turns to toast to their hoped-for success before filing out into the trench and pitch darkness.

23:50

The men on frontline duty have been told to expect the raiders both on their way out and return. They make space for the small party to pass and they clamber up the waiting ladder on to the parapet. From here, the men silently make their way to a shell hole in No Man's Land following white tape laid previously by a patrol. Here they position themselves in case they encounter an enemy patrol and wait for 'Zero Hour'.

The men choose their weapons carefully, knowing that they cannot take the 'soldier's friend' – the rifle – with them as it is simply too cumbersome, so pistols are hung around the neck and grenades stuffed in the pockets, allowing them to remain mobile as they travel through the enemy defences.

A mugful of rum helps to warm the men and perhaps perk them up, as although it is already nearly midnight, they have a long night in front of them.

The trench garrison have been warned of the raid and make preparations for the departure and return of the 'raiders'.

00:00

Seconds after midnight on the morning of 9 April, the British raiders leave the crater and head for the German frontline, invisible in the darkness. They move in two 'Indian files' one behind the other with the rearmost man checking behind them as they go. They are now on their own and have no idea what to expect on 'the other side'.

00:20

The first part of the raid has been uneventful. No shots have been fired and no flares have illuminated the raiders so far. In either event the plan is to freeze or remain static in the hope that they have not been spotted. Rifle fire and flares can be routine, or the result of a nervous and uncertain sentry. Recently, some German prisoners taken have been as young as 16 and they do not make good, steady soldiers.

00:40

The raiders have arrived, stealthily, at the German frontline trench having found gaps in the barbed wire which were partly concealed but numerous. They now wait just short of the parapet while one man looks into the enemy position. If there is no one in the trench, the rest will follow his lead.

01:00

The trench is empty and as men look each way down the trench, the others climb down into the deserted frontline. Their task is to look for defenders or evidence of who they might be.

01:20

Having reached a communication trench running to the rear without encountering any defenders, the raiders have a hurried conversation. Should they withdraw, although no signal has been given to do so, or press on deeper into the enemy position?

01:40

It has been decided that one group will remain in the German frontline trench to defend the escape route whilst the remainder explore the enemy communication trench (CT) to the second line. If anyone hears firing the party in the CT will withdraw to the frontline while the party there prevent the enemy from cutting them off.

01:50

The party in the CT has gone about 20 metres and there is still no sign of the occupants. Braziers they find are cold so there has been no one in the area since nightfall unless they are happy to be frozen. There are few souvenirs and even less information for the intelligence officers. So far, the raid has been a failure.

02:00

The party finds a dugout. Not deep, but there is a smell of cigarette smoke from the entrance and it might be occupied. Throwing in a couple of bombs would kill the occupants, but also alert every German in the area as to their presence and fail to get the information they need. The only option is for someone to go in and have a look.

02:10

The raid commander has decided that only he should take the risk of entering a dugout that might be occupied. Gripping a pistol with bayonet attached in his right hand and with an un illuminated torch in his left, he quietly enters the dugout entrance. His plan is to get inside and blind any occupants with the bright light while he decides to fight or flee. He holds the torch well to his left-hand side so that a shot from a defender might miss him.

02:20

The dugout is partly flooded and he is surprised at the amount of noise he makes as he stumbles into the pitch darkness. There is, however, no response from any other occupants. Standing in the doorway ready to grab a sleeping German, shoot or turn and run, he presses the button on top of his torch.

Armed with a pistol and bayonet attached, the raid commander is equipped for a close-quarters engagement.

02:30

The dugout is unoccupied. There is evidence that men had been there recently with a cigarette that had burned down to a butt, a guttering candle, an abandoned mug and some food debris. There is bedding on the bunks and a German helmet makes an excellent souvenir. However, nothing identifies the occupants of the dugout. There are no maps or papers and hence no evidence.

02:50

The search of the dugout has proved fruitless and the patrol sets off further down the CT in search of the information they need.

German helmets are a prized souvenir at the front with their distinctive design and raiding parties from both sides look for such items to take back across No Man's Land.

03:00

Just short of the German second line, a wooden and barbed-wire gate intended to halt raiders such as themselves blocks their passage. The gate is closed and may well be defended. Any attempt to simply open the gate may result in a volley of shots and flurry of grenades. With the raiders bunched in the trench, this could be a disaster. The raiders need to get round the gate and into the trench on the far side.

03:10

Using a trench board as an improvised ladder, the men climb out of the CT and through a gap in the barbed wire.

03:20

Still on the surface, the raiders check for defenders. There is no one in the CT or German second line. Empty enemy trenches suggest preparation for a gas attack or bombardment. They have instructions to be back in their own lines by 04:00 and speed is now essential. The disappointed patrol leader has no choice but to order his men back.

03:30

The men drop silently back into the CT and retrace their steps to the German frontline. It seems further on the way back than on the way out but they soon reach the rearguard party. The password is called for and the reply given and the two groups are reunited.

03:40

The return journey across No Man's Land is uneventful. Still no flares or shots and the watchful sentries in the British frontline are relieved to see 'their' raiders all return. No one has been lost.

03:50

The raiders gather in the dugout for a final drink of rum and the chance to compare stories. There is nothing to tell the intelligence officers other than they have found the enemy position empty. Could no news be good news? With their job done for the night warm straw in a barn behind the lines is a reward worth having for a few hours of tension and fear.

The men, exhausted by the tension of the last few hours, take stock for a few minutes; raids like this one could seem very high risk for little gain.

Portuguese infantry in France. (Official photograph, *The Times History of the War, Vol. XVIII*, 1919)

04:05

The men from No. 3 Section, 15 Platoon, 1/5th King's know that they are the left-hand battalion on the divisional front and that the junctions between adjoining units are always weak points. Some divisions in the British Army have good reputations and some bad, but the fact that the men in the line to their north are Portuguese does not inspire confidence. Known to one and all as the 'Pork and Beans', the turn out, drill and appearance of the soldiers from Britain's oldest ally is often a source of worry to those fighting alongside them. The platoon feel certain that 'their men' will put up a good fight, but that could not be said of their flank. The good news is that the handover between the men in the section is about to take place, although not on the

hour as this would be too obvious, and everyone is busy finding tools in the dark and getting a comfortable spot, even if that seems impossible. Others strip off warming cap comforters and balaclavas so that sentries can hear any threat from No Man's Land. The mist makes observation almost impossible and sentries strain to hear the click of weapons or movement in the wire that might betray an enemy patrol. Still nothing! The next hour will be even colder and men wriggle their toes inside boots to keep the circulation going as the temperature drops even lower.

A rumour has swept down the trenches that a patrol had ventured out earlier and had found the enemy trenches empty. This makes the men even more nervous. Sentries peer into the darkness determined not to miss any signs of attack.

04:15

At 04:15 exactly the bombardment from the enemy lines starts with a sudden crash that startles dozing men and sentries alike. The shells, however, do not crash down on the trenches. Instead, they hurtle high overhead to plunge into targets behind them. Quite where is not clear, but the men are not relieved. Are the enemy trying to cut them off from relief? An attack now might simply pin them in position. Unable to retreat or receive assistance from their supporting troops they would be on their own. As usual, there is no time to speculate; every man stands to and the order passed along to fix bayonets makes it clear that something is happening.

The 'Pork and Beans' – Portuguese infantry in the trenches. (Official photograph, *The Times History of the War, Vol. XVIII*, 1919)

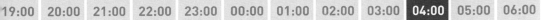

Sudden bombardments such as this one are disorientating; as the shells fall behind them, it is difficult for the men to ascertain what the target is and where the fire is coming from.

04:30

In the mist, some nameless gas sentry detects a whiff of gas and rattles, air horns, gongs and shouts of 'gas, gas, gas' alert every man to don his respirator. Helmets are knocked off and men fumble with their respirators, doing the drill by touch before flopping into the alert position on the fire step. Elsewhere gas curtains are closed, and braziers and stoves are extinguished so the flow of air that they encourage does not draw gas into the dugouts.

The gas sentry is a crucial role within the unit, alerting the men to the possibility of gas attack, and often known as 'canaries' as these birds were well known for their susceptibility to gas poisoning.

04:45

Whilst the men in the frontline stand to, the prearranged code word 'Bustle' is transmitted. On this, the reserve troops move to their battle positions in case of an enemy attack. All of this movement is unknown to those in the trenches and they spend lonely minutes isolated from each other by respirators, mist, darkness and, potentially, the threat of gas. Behind them men blunder to their positions also encumbered by respirators. The Germans are, indeed, using gas and it is drifting with the prevailing wind eastwards toward the frontline. This makes visibility worse and few people can see more than 20 metres in front of them.

At this point in the war gas is a known enemy and every man is familiar with gas drill and the respirator, but the claustrophobia and panic of a gas attack is something that it is impossible to become fully accustomed to.

05:00

It is critical to discover what is going on, and senior officers use every means possible to find out what the bombardment means. Experts have already reported that the gas is a mixture of varieties, but not of the most persistent type, 'Mustard Gas'. This means that the gas will clear readily allowing German troops to enter the affected area. What the gas does is to force the British troops to don their respirators. This restricts vision and makes physical work difficult. This is a major problem for the gunners as they sweat in their masks

It is hot and uncomfortable for troops whilst wearing a respirator and the confusion of battle makes it difficult to communicate or think clearly. Therefore one reason for using gas is not to kill your opponent – they will simply put on their respirators – but to make life difficult for them, slow them down and make work or decision-making very hard.

trying to load and fire their artillery pieces to counter the German bombardment. The German guns have the edge in terms of numbers and speed of loading and shells have cut many of the carefully laid telephone cables that are the only instantaneous means of communication between the frontline and headquarters. Signallers curse as lines go 'dis', or disconnected. This means not only will no messages get through but also that someone will have to venture out to find and repair the break.

06:00

The shelling has shifted to the communication trenches and most of the centres of resistance. Shells are falling behind them and there is no news from headquarters.

As shelling continues down the line the men alternate between standing guard and protecting themselves, keeping low in the trench or seeking better shelter.

06:45

The men in the trenches have been 'stood to' for two hours and although they can occasionally remove their respirators, they are tired, frustrated and worried. It is now fully daylight and the threat of a dawn attack has passed. The question on everyone's lips is will the Germans attack?

07:15

The level of German shelling has increased. Less gas, but more high-explosive shells. However, the main attention now appears to be to the north. The Portuguese are taking a pounding. Will it be the 1/5th King's turn next?

07:45

The first news arrives. Not from the rear but from a form of 'Chinese Whisper' down the frontline. The two companies of the battalion on the left have been overrun by a German attack and the enemy is now behind their left flank. With no orders to do otherwise, the men prepare to carry out their orders and hold on to the ground until help arrives.

Without real communications, trench whispers and rumours are inevitable in such situations. The men are tired and clearly no relief is in sight, so they know they must plan for what the day might bring.

Manoeuvrability in and out of the trenches is never easy and it is difficult for an attacker to do so unseen, but the 'fog of war' in this case aids the Germans.

08:30

Still no attack and no official news.

08:45

German troops are on the move. Using the mixture of fog and gas to provide cover they are closing on the British frontline. Well and lightly equipped for a mobile battle they have been provided with the best weapons available. They are confident of a victory that will end the war.

Shell holes are the only limited cover offered by No Man's Land.

09:00

Using the best cover available, German soldiers move across No Man's Land to close on the British defenders.

09:30

The German attackers are now in position and, following a bombardment from their own trench mortars, they will assault the British frontline.

09:50

Despite the lingering gas, bombardment and heavy German machine-gun and rifle fire, the defenders man their parapet as the Germans approach.

...ells burst across No Man's Land, leaving the defenders unclear as to the exact direction of the potential attack; all they ...e sure of is that they need to mount a defence and the platoon mans the fire step with their rifles.

The British catch glimpses of the attacking Germans through the smoke and the debris from their shell bursts. Howeve it is difficult to achieve accurate rifle fire in these circumstances. They are also inhibited by their gas masks, which tend to fog up and make normal breathing difficult.

The platoon operates a combined-arms approach, with the rifle section working alongside the bombers and rifle bombers to try to create a wall of fire to repel the Germans should they try to assault the position.

The rifle bomber in action; working alongside the conventional snipers of the platoon, the rifle bomber offers a wider range of firepower that is perhaps more suited to the situation where accuracy is almost impossible because of the confusion of the battle. Unlike snipers, who can only shoot at targets they can see, rifle bombers can also hit those who are taking cover. The grenades can be timed to 'air burst' so a shell hole or trench offers little protection.

Across No Man's Land, German riflemen return fire.

One disadvantage of the German MG08/15 'Light' machine gun is that it is water cooled and heavy. To make this worse, the water boils after about 1,000 rounds have been fired and at this point the machine-gunner finds the weapon almost too hot to touch.

10:15

The British response is surprising for the attackers. Despite the preparatory bombardment, the British are still in their positions and firing back. In a repeat of the British experience on the Somme and in later battles, shellfire cannot clear trenches of defenders. The German infantry will have to assault each position in turn.

10:30

Using the light version of the German Maxim machine gun, the MG08/15, German attackers target pockets of resistance. The weapon can fire over 600 bullets a minute and the result is devastating.

10:45

Under heavy fire from multiple weapons, the British defenders do their best to hold out, but simply cannot return fire without risking being hit.

11:00

With the Lewis gun jammed, the platoon commander has no choice other than to tell his men to retreat.

Opposite: The overwhelming firepower of the German attackers makes continued defence almost impossible.

Below: The platoon commander gives the order to withdraw.

As in all assaults, gaining intelligence about the enemy unit is vital and, although it was unpleasant for both sides to check through the uniform of a dead or wounded soldier, it was deemed a necessary evil to ensure the raid was a success. There also might be loot.

11:20

The Germans are in the British frontline trench and discover the body of a soldier killed in the recent attack. They check through his pockets for clues to identify the unit that they have overrun before they begin to move further into the trench system.

There is a marked difference in the rations fed to the British and the German soldiers, so the chance to feast on the British rations is not one to be missed. Looting was a common practice in trench raiding and raiders would vie with each other to claim superior souvenirs; helmets and battle insignia were among the most prized objects. However, by the spring of 1918 even frontline German soldiers are on 'short rations' and it is food that these men are in search of.

11:40

Having cleared the British trench, the attackers are distracted by loot. This was to be a pattern that was repeated in all the successful German attacks in the spring of 1918. Troops who had been hungry for months lost time and momentum when offered the opportunity to fill their haversacks with plentiful British foodstuffs.

The British troops retreat cautiously down the trench line, aware that the attackers are somewhere behind them. They aim for the support trench and hope to be able to stop the Germans at their barbed-wire anti-raid gate.

12:00

The British defenders have been forced back down their own communication trench. In a few places they are able to block the enemy attack, but in others cannot stem the tide. D Company work down Barnton Trench, putting up resistance as they go.

12:10 to 12:45

The German attack is relentless and despite the lifting of their supporting barrage to other targets, they are able to make progress towards the village of Festubert.

The Germans move down the trench line to clear out any remaining resistance.

Dugouts are systematically 'cleared' using grenades. A bomb down the steps kills or stuns the occupants.

The attackers, having cleared through the trench system, steadily make their way towards the village of Festubert, working round the flank of the King's Regiment.

13:00

There are many acts of gallantry by the defenders as they attempt to slow down or hold off the enemy attack. A sergeant from the platoon takes cover in a fresh shell hole and is successful in pinning down the Germans until he is hit in the lower arm. Unable to fire his weapon, he is captured whilst attempting to dress his wound. Many prisoners will be taken on both sides as the battle ebbs and flows.

A shell hole provides little cover for the defender, and risk of being hit and being taken prisoner as a consequence is high.

13:30

The British are now defending the outskirts of the village and here the hedges and walls provide ideal cover for the garrison. Elsewhere on the battlefield concrete shelters built into the strong points offer more protection for the defenders.

The British defenders use whatever cover they can find to mount a defence of the village.

13:45

The British defenders use everything possible to hold up the enemy attack and, where nature cover or trenches are absent, improvised barricades are built in lanes.

As the Germans advance they are unaware of the strong defence that has been formed in and around the village.

14:00

The attackers are still advancing in some places and some try shouting 'cease fire' in English to increase the confusion among the British.

14:20

Firing over open sights at targets only a few hundred yards away, British machine guns from the Machine Gun Corps (MGC) come into action. These weapons can fire over 550 bullets a minute and after years of indirect fire at targets the gunners could not see the men of the MGC are able to identify plenty of targets as the enemy attempt to close on the village.

The Vickers machine gun is the staple of the Machine Gun Corps. Water cooled and heavy, it can deliver sustained fire at long range. The enemy is now close and, although they are using whatever cover is available, the men of the 'Emma Gees' carry out their task with a will. Most men of the MGC have not seen targets like this ever before.

14:30

The Germans find that their attacks are taking increasingly heavy casualties and that the advance is slowing. By now, the 55th Division's headquarters have reinforced the defence with all available infantry, but also the cooks, clerks and spare men are mobilised to defend the village.

14:45

British soldiers attempt to dig in on unpromising positions. Even a shallow hole can make a man a smaller target and men dig in with entrenching tools, spades and anything else that can move the soft clay. Conditions are more like 1914 than traditional trench warfare.

German rifles – even with the support of a few automatic weapons – are now beginning to find that they are outmatched by the British firepower.

Digging in was one method to establish a defensive perimeter and shore up a position gained or to be held on to.

15:00

With increasing numbers of British troops in action, the German advance is slowing. In some areas British artillery are forced to fire their guns over open sights and the gunners use their rifles and Lewis guns to defend the gun pits.

15:30

A number of British defenders have been taken prisoner. These men are now searched and disarmed before being sent further back by their captors. Treatment is good, although a few Germans who are frustrated by the stubborn defence 'rough up' some prisoners.

In this battle prisoners on both sides receive relatively good treatment. The first job of any soldier taking prisoners is to establish their unit and rank; this then determined how useful they would be for intelligence on enemy positions and plans.

15:45

By late afternoon, the casualties from the early fighting have made their way to their Regimental Aid Post in the frontline and then back to a variety of Advance Dressing and Casualty Clearing Stations. Here their wounds are reassessed to ensure that they are sufficiently fit to be sent to the hospitals well behind the lines.

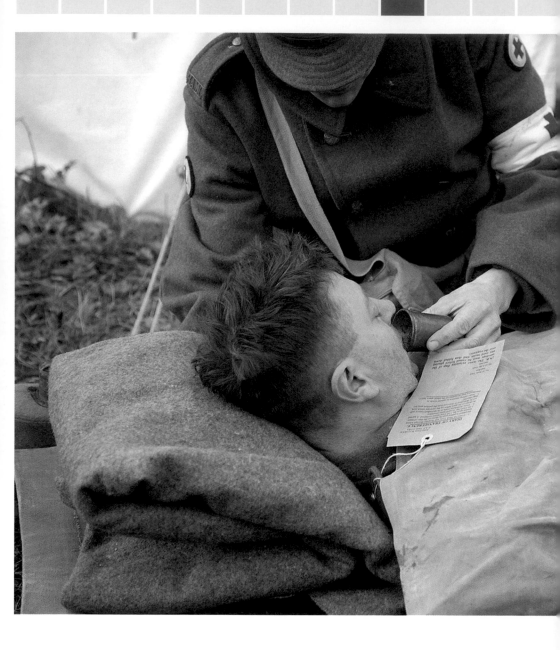

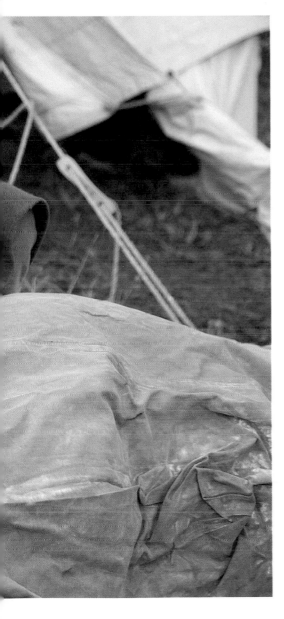

The wounded platoon commander, rescued in the fighting, receives treatment. His wound will be assessed and then he will be sent back to a Casualty Clearing Station depending on the severity. Some soldiers longed for a 'Blighty wound', enabling them to be sent home for rest and respite.

16:00

Some casualties have received gunshot injuries, but the majority have been hit by fragments from German mortar bombs and shells. A few are suffering from the effects of gas. One of the most famous photographs of the war shows men from the 55th Division blinded by gas. This photograph was taken at a Casualty Clearing Station during the April fighting. Most would recover their sight, but they were out of the battle, which is what the Germans wanted.

Gas attacks leave lingering injuries, blindness being the most common and most frightening. Blind casualties are escorted to the Dressing Station for immediate treatment before being removed behind the lines. The majority will make a full recovery, but their plight is clear.

16:30

Across the battlefield, individually and in small knots where men had fought and died together, there are bodies. Most have already been looted of valuables and the area is now scattered with discarded weapons and equipment, but also with letters and documents thrown away by the looters.

17:00

Before darkness begins to fall men assess the situation by peering out into No Man's Land through their trench periscopes, trying to establish just what remains of the enemy forces on the other side.

Putting one's head above the parapet to take a peek across No Man's Land was a risky business; the trench periscope is designed to allow the sniper or rifleman a better view to the enemy positions on the other side without necessarily alerting the enemy to his presence. Once it is dark the sentry will have to lean over the parapet and trust his life to luck.

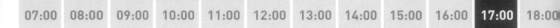

The men take stock of their positions, exhausted, but confident of having repelled the worst of the attack.

18:00

Both sides have virtually fought themselves to a standstill. The Germans are exhausted, demoralised about their lack of success and unsure of their own positions or those of the British. The British defenders are no less tired; it has been a very long day, but it is clear that they still largely hold the ground they were instructed to defend.

19:00

As the evening draws in, men find time to eat and have a drink.

20:00

The platoon is assigned to their various positions, so that the 'normal' trench routine of watch, repair and rest is re-established.

Trench revetting is hard work and although it seems ludicrous to carry it out at night after a battle, when urgent repairs must be made there is no choice. Such works are dangerous though as they can alert the enemy to activity on the other side and incur rifle fire or worse.

21:00

Despite their tiredness, there can be no rest for some as the day's action has damaged defences that must be urgently repaired.

22:00

Those on stand-to have to remain alert for further raids and reprisals that might occur throughout the night.

22:45

Some grab a few moments of much-needed rest after the continuous fighting of the day. Others simply reflect on the day's activities and the men that have been injured, taken prisoner or those who won't be coming back.

CONCLUSION

The Duke of Wellington described the Battle of Waterloo as 'a near run thing'. The same can be said of the defence of the Givenchy to Festubert line by the 55th Division in April 1918. When the Portuguese Division collapsed during the early morning of 9 April, they were left with their flank 'in the air'. The Old British Line (OBL) was abandoned and the Germans swept through the gap heading west. This meant that there were no friendly troops on their left and that the German attackers had the opportunity to get behind their position. If this had occurred the division would have faced attack from front and rear. Cut off and surrounded, it is likely that they would have been destroyed and the German attack would have swept on as intended. In reality, the men of the division fought gallantly, repulsing the German attacks on their own front and causing heavy casualties on their assailants. At the same time they formed an improvised 'refused flank' turned back like a hairpin so that the troops faced east, north and north-west at one point. The Germans had not realised how close to victory they had come and the ferocity of the British defence prevented them from fully exploiting their initial success. The files of The National Archives in Kew are full of carefully collected after-battle reports, many by very junior officers in the 55th Division, in which they describe in detail their experiences during the German onslaught. These make compelling reading and convey a little of the drama that unfolded.

A brigade report is matter of fact about the position that followed the collapse of the Portuguese and the dangers this caused:

> The OBL [Old British Line] was heavily attacked and its flank turned by Germans advancing from the North and getting behind the garrison. The Portuguese has by this time disappeared and the whole of our flank was exposed. An officer who had been sent to see what was happening tried to rally them until the Portuguese threatened to bayonet him.

An officer reports the attack on his position around noon on 9 April:

> A few minutes later a few single Germans approached the post,
> followed by several detached parties, not more than twelve to
> a party. The machine guns and rifles played havoc. Those of the
> enemy who did not fall disappeared back into the mist. One of
> the parties brought a light machine gun to fifteen yards of the
> post. The Germans were killed and the gun taken in during the
> night following.

A second officer describes a later attack that was dealt with even
more effectively. The much-reported 'storm troop' tactic appears to
have totally failed in this assault:

> At 3pm the shelling ceased, and six Companies appeared on the
> right bombing their way up the trench covered by riflemen in the
> rear. The bombers were driven out and killed, and the riflemen
> killed in the rear ... Capt. Russell sent reinforcements of 1 Sgt.
> (Sgt Carruthers) and right men to protect my flanks [and] rear and
> to provide better infantry personnel for the machine gun and at
> 10 pm sec Lieut J V Wheeler and fourteen other ranks from 13 and
> 16 Platoons arrived. These provided standing and reconnoitring
> patrols all round the post during the night and a standing patrol in
> the rear in daytime to prevent a recurrence of the above incident.

Another officer appears quite relaxed about the position in which his
platoon found itself:

> About midday I observed enemy 400 yards away in attack
> formation, they were advancing from Route A Keep. I
> immediately opened Lewis gun fire on them and sent runners
> to Bn. H.Qrs Cailloux Keep and to Machine gunners on my left.
> Enemy were easily beaten off by the machine Gun, Lewis gun
> and rifle fire brought to bear on them, and retired in disorder.

Although the position took days to stabilise, the German attack
on the Lys front was ultimately a failure. They suffered significant

casualties and though they succeeded in advancing into the British position in some areas this break was quickly sealed off by a variety of reinforcements. For a while artillerymen fought in hand-to-hand combat and men used to working behind the lines found themselves serving as riflemen. One of the most noticeable factors in the accounts of this period of fighting, which is borne out by the accounts above, is the high level of confidence among the British defenders despite the very difficult position in which they found themselves. It is also clear that commanders could rely on men from a variety of units even if they were not necessarily serving under their 'own' officers or NCOs. This ability is rightly regarded as a very important military attribute and we can gauge the professionalism that the men of the British Army had achieved by 1918 from their performance in this battle.

The battle of April 1918 was not the end of the war for the 55th Division and they participated in the advance, which started in August and ended on 11 November as the Armistice came into effect ending the war on the Western Front. At that time, the division had advanced 50 miles over the previous eighty days. This is not the most remarkable advance of any division in the British Army in the '100 Days' from August to November 1918, but it serves to indicate the mobile nature of warfare at the end of the campaign in the west.

BIBLIOGRAPHY

Primary Sources

Instructions for the Training of Platoons for Offensive Action, 1917, SS 143, General Staff, 1917

Military Operations: France and Belgium, 1917, compiled by Brigadier-General Sir James E. Edmonds (London: HMSO, 1940)

Military Operations: France and Belgium, 1918, Vol. 1, compiled by Brigadier-General Sir James E. Edmonds (London: HMSO, 1935)

Military Operations: France and Belgium, 1918, Vol. 2, compiled by Brigadier-General Sir James E. Edmonds (London: HMSO, 1937)

The Training and Employment of Platoons 1918, SS 143, General Staff, 1918

War Diary of 165 Brigade (Kew: The National Archives)

War Diary of 1/5th King's Liverpool Regiment (Kew: The National Archives)

Secondary Sources

Baker, Chris, *The Battle for Flanders: German Defeat on the Lys 1918* (Pen and Sword, 2011)

Brown, Malcolm, *The Imperial War Museum Book of 1918: Year of Victory* (Sidgwick and Jackson, 1998)

Hart, Peter, *1918: A British Victory* (Weidenfeld and Nicolson, 2008)

Kitchen, Martin, *The German Offensive of 1918* (Tempus, 2001)

Middlebrook, Martin, *The Kaiser's Battle* (Allen Lane, 1978)

Sheffield, Gary, *Forgotten Victory: The First World War: Myths and Realities* (Headline, 2001)

Tomaselli, Phil, *Battle of the Lys 1918, Givenchy and the River Law* (Pen and Sword, 2011)

ABOUT THE PHOTOGRAPHER

PaGe Images is a father and daughter photography team consisting of Phil and Georgee Erswell.

Phil has been taking photographs for over thirty years both as a hobby and professionally. The professional side started after he was asked to photograph a friend's wedding twenty years ago. After that more requests started coming in and he was soon working as a part-time wedding and portrait photographer. On retiring from the Metropolitan Police after thirty years' service, he became a full-time professional photographer concentrating on events and weddings: 'Georgee and myself work well together. At weddings Georgee concentrates on the informal reportage portraits while I get on with the required shots. At events I take the images while Georgee sells & prints the images.'

When not working as a photographer Phil spends his time touring and researching the Great War, a passion that has developed over the last fifteen years. Some of Phil's images taken in France and Belgium can be seen on his other site at www.barbedwiretours.co.uk.

If you enjoyed this book, you may also be interested in…

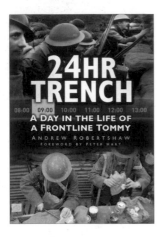

24hr Trench
ANDREW ROBERTSHAW

The trench was the frontline Tommy's home. He ate, slept, and sometimes died in this narrow passage amongst the slime of mud and blood on the Western Front. Millions of men died on both sides during the war and whilst serving in the trenches – but how did they live in them? First World War historian Andrew Robertshaw and a group of soldiers, archaeologists and historians use official manuals and diaries to build a real trench system and live in it for 24 hours, recreating the frontline Tommy's daily existence. Hour by hour, the Tommy's day unfolds through stunning colour photographs in this ground-breaking experiment in Great War history.
978 0 7524 7667 4

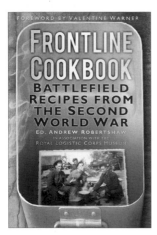

Frontline Cookbook
ED. ANDREW ROBERTSHAW

Frontline Cookbook brings together recipes from the Second World War, including hand-written notes from troops fighting in the Middle East, India and all over Europe. Many recipes are illustrated with cartoons and drawings on how to assemble the perfect oven and kitchen tools at a moment's notice from nothing. This book is the perfect inspiration for those who like to create an amazing meal anywhere, anytime, from anything.

978 0 7524 7665 0

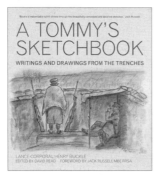

A Tommy's Sketchbook
LANCE-CORPORAL HENRY BUCKLE, ED. DAVID READ

During his time on the Ypres Salient Lance-Corporal Buckle kept a diary and sketchbook. He was a keen amateur photographer and water-colourist. Together with his diary, Henry Buckle's paintings, over sixty in number, provide a fascinating insight into life in and out of the trenches in France during 1915. Contemporary colour images from the front are all too rare, and Henry's charming and naïve pictures are full of exquisite details and insights.

978 0 7524 6605 7

Visit our website and discover thousands of other History Press books.
www.thehistorypress.co.uk